# MORE PRAISE FOR
# CATHERINE AUMAN

"For those readers, men and women, who wish to enrich their love lives, investigating Catherine's sage and well-considered advice could be just the answer and the path you're looking for!"

— *Osho Times*, international online magazine

"For many years there have been books about how to be tricky, guarded, or false in the world of dating by "the rules." Thank goodness that Catherine Auman has spelled out a different and better way. This is a book for people who want integrity, authenticity, and genuine connection to truly happen. It's a much-needed approach that feels both new and timeless."

— Leonard Felder, PhD, author of
*Fitting in is Overrated*

D0916646

"I love this book. Thank you, Catherine Auman. If you haven't read or don't know anything about the tantric approach to dating, check out this book and consider attending one of Catherine's workshops—truly game changing."

— Carina Eriksson, Professional Matchmaker

"The book *Tantric Dating* offers much-needed clarity and insight into the world of sacred sexuality and the much-bantered term "tantra". The author is the real deal and she teaches that love is always available and changing our perception is an important place to begin."

— Corey Folsom, Sex & Relationship Coach

"When it comes to dating coaching, I would completely trust Catherine Auman and welcome her perspective."

— Vince Kelvin, Seminar Leader and Coach

# Tantric Relating

## Relationship Advice to Find and Keep Sex, Love and Romance

### Catherine Auman, LMFT

Green Tara Press

Green Tara Press

Los Angeles, CA

www.greentarapress.com

"Envisioning Your Lover as the God or Goddess They Truly Are" and "What Do We Mean by Spiritual Relationships" were previously published in Catherine Auman's book *Shortcuts to Mindfulness: 100 Ways to Personal and Spiritual Growth*.

© 2022 Catherine Auman

All Rights Reserved.

Auman, Catherine I.

Tantric Relating: Relationship Advice to Find and Keep Sex, Love and Romance

Self Help 2. Dating 3. Spiritual

ISBN 978-1-945085-28-4 Paperback

ISBN 978-1-945085-29-1 Electronic Book Text

Author Photo by Charity Burnett

Cover Art by Katrina Pacheco

Back Cover and Interior Book Design by Lilly Penhall

# CONTENTS

# INTRODUCTION

We relate differently when the Other is the Beloved.

Compare: In contemporary culture, the other person is frequently seen as an enemy or someone to compete with or be jealous of. The other is someone you can't trust and must play skillful games with if you want to get ahead. You've studied ways to improve communication because you're into personal and spiritual growth, but you haven't found what's out there as helpful as you hoped because, as in conventional dating and mating, the underlying premise beneath the conventional worldview will never work. Tantra offers the antidote to all this disease, a radical perspective on relating.

With all the talking going on out there it seems as if we must be relating, but our results show otherwise. With over half of all relationships calling it quits, with nations and tribes at war, and with simple civility toward our fellow humans taking a nosedive—perhaps the way we are relating is contributing to a crisis in communication rather than making things better.

As a person serious about personal and spiritual growth, you may have experienced relating as a major challenge—it is for most people. You may have felt that you were talking too much or too little, that you need to keep who you are hidden away, concealing the extent of your hopes and dreams, or that you were being too bold or too shy. This confusion showed up in your romantic life as secrets, lots of crying, broken trust, and in the end, the death of the coupledom. You kept reading self-help books and online articles, but rapport with would-be partners spiraled quickly downward.

You've most likely tried being a positive, upbeat person, not sharing things that your partner might not like. You've even experimented with mind-reading and subterfuge. You've kept your opinions and unhappiness to yourself, or shared them only with your therapist and friends. The fights and blowups inexplicably continued.

As a Licensed Marriage and Family Therapist working with individuals and couples, I've noticed that conventional suggestions for improving communication don't help much. Active listening, still prescribed by therapists and coaches, has been scientifically proven not to work[1]. Scheduling special times to talk, practicing positivity, writing down criticisms, women speaking in different ways than men—when we remember to do these actions they might help, but when we forget, things get worse; and they're hard to remember in the heat of things. These conventional techniques, while well-intended, do not stem the bleeding.

It was the tantric perspective that changed everything for me, as it was in dating and mating. In tantra, everything is perfect in this moment, so what is true in the present is welcome, even if it's hard. It's also the tantric perspective that whoever is in front of you in this moment is the Beloved, your chance to experience love or not, and that it is up to you, not the other person.

I didn't understand the extent to which conventional ideas about relating were having a negative effect on my relationships until I met my Perfect Beloved, now husband, Greg Lawrence. Greg had experienced the devastation of conventional relating in his previous partnerships, and he was craving something different this time. Together, we pieced out what we wanted for our partnership, and it has been working so well that we can honestly say that our relationship is light-years beyond what we ever imagined for ourselves.

I don't think it's on anyone's relationship goals list to sit and stew in silence, or to experience those excruciating conversational log jams. We all long for someone with whom we can talk freely and have our ideas and enthusiasms warmly received. We crave living in an atmosphere of total trust and safety, and to luxuriate in a frequency of love and support. And what about the world of nonverbal communication? In tantra we are all about the body, so that must be addressed as well.

This book, *Tantric Relating*, is about how you can communicate both verbally and non- to keep the love fires burning, and to find and keep the sex, love and romance of your dreams. In *Tantric Dating*, the secrets of why you haven't found love and how to find it are explained. *Tantric Mating* illuminates how to be in partnership and create your perfect soulmate relationship. In this book, you'll learn how to make agreements about truth sharing, how to know when an issue is resolved, how and why to clear all resentments, how to praise, thank and flirt, and why "When in doubt, touch."

The teachings in this book can change all your relationships, not just the one with your Beloved. Yes, you can use these principles to create the love affair of your dreams. After that, or while you're waiting, please join us in applying them widely to help the world blossom into an oasis of love.

1   Gottman, John and Gottman, Julie Schwartz. *Gottman Method Couples Therapy: Bridging the Couple Chasm*. The Gottman Institute, 2012

# TANTRIC RELATING MINDSET

# To Tell the Truth or Not, That Is the Question

We're taught from an early age not to speak our truth. We'll get in trouble if we do, or we'll be spanked, shamed, or isolated. We learn to sit quietly and behave. Of course, it's good not to let children run around screaming in restaurants or tell Uncle Joe that he smells funny, so part of this shaping of personalities is mastering how to coexist with other people. However, the brainwashing has begun: it's not safe to speak your truth.

Girls are socialized to not offer our opinions in class, to not appear too smart, and to always act in a pleasing manner. Boys are brainwashed to never feel or express feelings, including not crying, and to appear as though they don't give a damn. Of course, if you don't identify as strictly male or female you are SOL. People of color are expected to adopt the dominant worldview without complaint, and old people, well, old people should just shut up and fade away.

In the workplace, even though many bosses state they want an open environment where people can speak freely, only the most naive would take them at their word. The modern dating market is rife with "expert" advice on how to tangle one's words around to manipulate others into desiring us. Most of us have no idea how much we've been hypnotized to accept the mainstream's version of us as ourselves, or how to find or locate our personal truth.

It's good that we learn how to conform and not share too much of our personal selves in the social and work spheres. If we want to be successful, these are necessary skills. However, in intimate partnerships, the opposite is true. The problem is that people get into love relationships with no understanding that speaking their own truth and being open to the truth of their partner(s) is what creates intimacy and connection.

With all this training to NOT tell the truth about ourselves, how are we supposed to suddenly BE our true selves in relationships?

Humming along underneath all this socialization and programming of how to be successful in the world is the heartbeat of tantra. Tantra teaches us that everything is perfect in the present moment; therefore, whatever your or your partner's personal truth is is part of that perfection, even if it creates difficulty. You would want to express your truth, and you would want your partner to express their truth. In tantra, everything is divine, so every feeling that you have and share with your partner would be divine as well.

When you enter into a relationship inspired by tantric principles, you and your partner will be encouraged to share your complete and honest truth with each other. You'll see: it makes for great sex and intimacy.

# Permission to Be Unkind

We all say things we wish we hadn't. Maybe you were a little more curt or not as caring as you would like to have been. Perhaps you realize you've been sarcastic or cutting. Sometimes you don't realize your part until later when you're wondering how that fight began. Relating does not go as hoped often due to our human frailties, so when it's been with a person you're close to, it's good to check in and see, "Is that something I'd say to my boss, co-worker, or friend?" If it's not, it's important to admit that you gave yourself permission to be unkind.

This is normally when someone responds, "Well, I couldn't help it," or "I was all stressed out," or "The other person was being a @%#&." The fact is, nearly everyone has the ability to not make out-of-control comments to people in authority. You would take care to never talk rudely to your boss, for example.

You edit yourself for police and in social situations, so this idea that "I couldn't help it" really doesn't hold weight.

Becoming aware of and getting over giving ourselves permission to be unkind is an inside job. It's not about the other person and that what they've done is irritating or triggering. It's about "Do I want to grow myself up so I'm not a person who gives myself permission to say unkind things?" You make an internal decision to raise your own standards of behavior. You want to take responsibility so that these mean statements don't stick and have a permanent effect on your relationship, and the other person isn't injured because you spouted off.

There are certain things that only an intimate partnership brings up. You may have been working on yourself diligently, but as soon as you enter a relationship, boom, your neglected inner child comes out. Sometimes because of our unresolved past, we might feel like letting ourselves go and acting like a two-year-old. This may be a challenge, especially if you grew up in a sometimes unkind home, but it's worth the effort to change because you become a person who never speaks hurtfully.

There's the added fact that when you let yourself go and say inconsiderate things, terrible self-esteem follows, and in a way that's right because why should we feel good about less-than-loving behavior? It's time to remind yourself that even if you're not perfect, you're working earnestly at becoming as kind and compassionate as you aspire to be. This kind of personal work is advantageous for you, your partner, your relationship, and the greater community. The whole world benefits from kind, evolving individuals and happy couples.

# Don't Rock the Boat, Baby

"Rock the Boat" was the name of a worldwide disco hit back in the '70s. The infectious chorus repeated, "Rock the boat, don't rock the boat, baby," over and over. It's said that every minute of the day that song is playing somewhere in the world. A friend of mine's uncle wrote it, and apparently, he lived high all his life on the royalties from that one song.

A fun song but maybe not the best relationship advice. Another issue that can sink the ship of relationships is that "Don't rock the boat" is a strategy many couples use as they attempt to navigate their relating: Don't talk about that difficult thing! It'll create more trouble! You're not supposed to talk about stuff like that. Don't rock the boat because it will make your partner unhappy. You smile, say nothing's wrong when it obviously is, and refuse to discuss the thing that's bugging you.

You may have the best intentions, but all that unspoken communication begins to pile up and create congestion on the high seas. The problems don't go away; in fact, they multiply because nothing is getting solved. It shows up in the bedroom as "I'm not in the mood." Yes, it's difficult to bring up the topic that your sex life has gotten stale, but do you think your partner hasn't noticed?

If you or your partner are arguing a lot, or are not using loving language, don't you think both of you are unhappy? Yes, there are many things you can bring up that are going to make your partner uncomfortable, but that is part of how we grow.

A commonly used metaphor is that each person in a relationship is wearing a backpack, and everything that doesn't get discussed is a rock that gets stored back there. Little by little as rocks keep being added with each topic not discussed, the load gets heavier and heavier until one day, one person throws the contents of their backpack out on the table, and all hell breaks loose.

Juicy, alive relationships require having their boat rocked. Unless you want to end up as one of those couples sitting in restaurants not talking to each other, bored with life, you'll need to share what's going on with you, getting into complete agreement and honesty. Honesty sometimes leads to difficulty. Part of tantric relating is making agreements with your partner that you *will* rock the boat. Anything that's not talked about is going to eventually cause holes in your boat and make it impossible for you to have the rich, erotic sex, love and romance that your soul longs for.

# The Spiritual Path
# of Relating

If you realized that the person sitting in front of you was your Beloved, how would you treat them? I suspect it would be with kindness and love. You would focus on their strengths and good points and ignore what you perceive to be the less-so. (After all, that's how we treat our friends, right?) You'd speak carefully and tenderly and attend to their comfort. You'd feel grateful that love has shown up for you and count your blessings. And maybe, just maybe, you'd be aware of the divine spark at the core of that other person's being, silently blazing away, equal to the one inside you.

But, your mind says, this person isn't flawless enough to be my perfect partner. This person is— fill in the blank—not good looking enough, they've gained weight, they're too messy or too much of a neatnik, they don't have sex as often or as little as you do and when they do it's not the right way to get you off. If you observe carefully, you'll notice that your mind wants to itemize every "wrong" thing about this person as an explanation for why they aren't your perfect love. The mind doesn't like the idea that anyone but a fantasy figure is the Beloved, so it rejects the real human being and closes your heart.

You've been taught by the conventional culture that love exists sometime in the future when you'll meet and get involved with a perfect person, or that love is only to be given to people who look and act a certain way. In tantra, we learn that if we can't relate to the person in front of us with love and awareness, we won't be available for love with our romantic partner either.

Early in my work with one of my mentors, he told me that he relates to a homeless person on a bench the same way he treats a fashion model. Most of us would treat one of those people with derision and disrespect and the other with adulation and fawning behavior. At that moment my mentor's near-sainthood in relating to other beings became clear to me, and I have forever more aspired to that level of respect and tantric relating.

An elevating ideal, perhaps, but difficult in practice? Yes, but worth pursuing as we turn ourselves into lovers. When we practice relating to everyone as an emanation of the divine, we gain skill in the art of relating to our partner. Tantra is about seeing sex, love and romance as part of the spiritual path, and everyone we encounter is an opportunity for practice.

The first step in tantric relating is that relating to others becomes an essential element of your spiritual path, one of the major avenues for expressing our love in the world. All little moments between you and another are opportunities to practice becoming a more loving person. Every encounter with another is an encounter with the divine.

You can begin today relating in the tantric way by realizing that whomever you are with right now is a divine being, and it is up to you to recognize it. Relate to everyone as someone you love, most not in the romantic sense, but in a spirit of camaraderie as spiritual brothers and sisters helping each other grow. The more you practice with everyone you meet, the more your heart will open and become accustomed to sharing love in every moment.

# Relating Through the Body

Tantra is all about being in the body. Conventional culture insists we live our lives in our heads: thinking, analyzing, judging. Most of us don't even like our bodies very much. We've been taught (relentlessly) by social media and advertising that our bodies are not shaped right, and that we need to aspire to be different. Our bodies may carry memories of past trauma we'd like to forget. We've become more comfortable watching life with our eyes and brains, instead of participating in the often-messy IRL.

Most of us have no idea that we're not IN our bodies. It wasn't until I lived at the tantra ashram that I learned there was another way. I had always assumed I was in my body because I was a dancer, did yoga, and ate healthy, but at the ashram I learned that these were things I was doing TO my body.

Not that there's anything wrong with trying to be healthy and fit, but I had never asked my body if these were routines it wanted or enjoyed. I'd been forcing disciplines on it, some of which in the long run turned out to be unhealthy.

When we relate tantrically, we acknowledge that we live in bodies. Not the perfect, airbrushed online images, but living, breathing, conscious bodies. Bodies that don't always smell good or do what we want them to. When your body's enlivened by practicing embodiment exercises and awareness practices, you become attentive to the fact that your physical self is never not communicating. The body is sharing your aliveness, or enthusiasm, or lack of sleep. It communicates its delicious desire, or fear or blockages. You become willing to learn from its wisdom.

Tantric relating is through the fingertips, the breath, the sounds, and the soul. Psychologists say that only seven percent of communication is verbal. If you live in your head you miss most of what is being related. What is your body saying? What does a hand on your shoulder mean, or a kiss on the forehead? Arms folded protecting the heart? What do you communicate about respect for the other person when you ask permission before giving a hug?

Our bodies long for touch. You might even feel touch starved—no shame there—many people, if not most, do. Often reaching out and sharing touch speaks way more than words. When you're embodied and relate through the physical, are not ashamed of your body, comfortable with expressing physical affection, your vibe will be one of love.

Clear, open tantric relating will be enhanced when we clear our shame about our bodies, past abuse, fears about being touched, loved, being intimate. Fears that we love too much, that the other person will leave us or laugh at us, that our love will not be reciprocated. When you work with and move past these fears you'll be able to touch without shame, fear, embarrassment, or concern about sexual performance.

If you are deeply relating to your own body, you will be open and excited to communicate with your lover's body. Bodies by themselves, when cleared of mental chatter and resentments, want to make love, and they don't want to stop. One person with a healed body meets another person with a healed body: this is one of the elements that contributes to tantric sex being as good as you've heard it is.

# Agreements to Talk about Everything

One of the reasons we choose to relate differently in a tantric relationship is because we want to keep the energy clear between us. Only then can we have beautiful tantric sex, because only then can we exist in a blissful climate free of resentments, anger, and fights. If you are mad at your partner, unhappy with them, or in a snit, you will be unhappy in your life and your lovemaking, if it exists at all, will be unsatisfying. To say the least.

Making an agreement to talk about everything creates a safe ambiance, strengthening the climate of trust in your relationship so that you won't ever have to worry that your partner is keeping something from you. To agree to talk about everything means you know you can speak your mind and the other person isn't going to freak out, accuse you of misdeeds, or call you names.

In previous relationships, there were probably many things you couldn't talk about. For example, you didn't know for certain how your partner was feeling but it felt risky to ask, or they would just answer "fine" when you knew they weren't. You had a gut feeling they weren't happy, but they wouldn't talk about it so you weren't sure. You suspected they were flirting with other people on social media; perhaps it turned out to be true. But you weren't able to bring these things up, because it seemed better to keep from rocking the boat.

In a relationship where an agreement has been made to talk about everything, you would already have permission to ask, "Hey, how are you feeling?" or "Are you less happy with our relationship than you used to be? How would you like us to change?" And your partner would feel free to answer, "Yes, I'd like more physical affection. Seems like we used to have that more, and I miss it." Whatever the truth might be, you can talk about it. The issues are out in the open and don't have to be hidden, hitting you unsuspectingly when they come to light.

I saw a patient the other day who was trying to express what he wanted to do on vacation, and his partner called him a snob for his desire to spend the night at an expensive resort. Being put down like that obviously doesn't help the conversation move forward. This name-calling made it unsafe for him to bring up his wants and desires for fear of being ridiculed.

Having an agreement to talk about everything also means conversations may get difficult sometimes. In tantra, since the entire world is held as sacred, every emotion would be sacred too. There is nothing that would not be, so we would welcome difficult feelings, arguments, misunderstandings—all are part of our personal and spiritual growth. Living with an agreement to talk about everything will be worth any challenges because of the great freedom it creates, the freedom to bring your full self to the relationship so you can be truly loved as you are.

Thus one of the foundational steps in tantric relating is to have a conversation with your partner about whether or not you want to make such an agreement. How much truth do you want to share? How much freedom do you and your partner want to live in? Are you willing to hear their truth? Make your version of the agreement together—even dar-

ing to have the discussion will evolve your relationship to new depth.

# The Process of Clearing

Everything you haven't talked about is going to show up in the bedroom. It's bound to appear as "I don't feel like it" or "I'm not in the mood" or you wondering why three months have gone by since the two of you made love. When you're carrying a grudge, even if it's over something tiny and supposedly insignificant, you won't feel like getting intimate. And who can blame you?

That's why it's important, if you want great relating and a great sex life, to have an agreement not only to talk about everything, but also to clear things as soon as you're aware there's an issue. What does that mean? Here's an example:

You're taking a morning walk together, and you notice you're feeling a bit uncomfortable. Instead of ignoring it, you look inside and assess that you're anxious because your partner said something sharply at breakfast, and you've felt a bit miffed ever since. So, with the permission to bring things up, you would ask, "May I bring something up?" (It's always a good idea to make sure this is a good time so as to not ambush them.) "I'm still not done about the disagreement we had this morning. I felt you spoke to me in a harsh way that wasn't justified. Do you feel I am overreacting?"

And your partner might reply, "Oh, no, sorry. I was a tired and, I guess, grumpy. I was thinking about something I read in the news that triggered me, so no, I'm not upset with you. Thanks for asking."

Right there, you're not going home all worried that they're mad at you, or that you said something stupid. You know how the mind can go on and on that maybe what you said ruined things. The monkey mind can create all kinds of scenarios to torture us if we don't stop in the moment and check things out with the other person.

You may have had previous relationships where the smallest thing would trigger World War III. If you don't bring issues up, little blips of resentment expand and multiply and before you know it, someone leaves the refrigerator door open and there's a huge skirmish that has nothing to do with the fridge—it's about all the minor issues that have built up over time. So, if you don't want that type of relating, you'll get to the point where you'll be happy to bring things up, because you don't want to be carrying them forward, affecting your mood, your motivation level, a lack of emotional comfort, or whether or not you feel secure in your relationship.

Firstly, agree to bring things up to be cleared. Secondly, discuss as soon as possible, although later is better than never. Lastly, talk about whatever is between you until both people feel satisfied. When you clear things in the moment, perfect love reappears. You've returned to that lovely river of energy that connects you. That's always the goal, to get back to that pure stream of love, flowing like water.

# Clearing the Past

Many couples' relationships are trapped in layers of resentment. The lovers are still unfinished or mad about things that happened a year ago, five years ago, maybe even twenty depending on the length of the relationship. When a couple has gotten into trouble or is not making love any more, there's usually much excavating of the past that needs to be done in order to thrive together in the present moment.

Spiritual traditions have a long history of methods for an individual to clear their past. For example, in Toltec shamanism, there's a process in which you list every incident that has happened in your life and then clear and clean it. Twelve-step programs include the Fourth Step where you make a list of everyone you've felt resentment toward in your life, you take responsibility for your part in the upset, and then release it by sharing with a trusted advisor.

In another tradition, the process is called *clearing*, where you go back to everything in the past that still has "charge" on it. The results of this clearing process are actually read on a meter to measure whether or not your issue is complete. Psychotherapy attempts to clear traumatic incidents in the past that are still causing distress.

What does this mean that you clear the past until you don't "have charge on it" anymore? It means: If your body is still responding to the memory of the event, you are not done. Do you still cry, does your breath stop, do feelings come up into your heart or make you feel sick to your stomach? These are all indications that the issue has not been cleared. In your work on yourself as an individual, you process these memories until there's no more upset about anything from your past. Anything that's not clear, anything you're still afraid or ashamed of, anything that you've not forgiven yourself for or feel sad about will show up not only in not having the best life possible, but also as challenges in your relationships.

For couples this means going back and clearing all memories of upset, which can be a lengthy process. Every incident from the past that hasn't been cleared is going to show up as difficulty in the present moment. If there are still resentments, it's going to show up in the bedroom.

It's an archaeological excavation, rooting these things out, talking them through until neither of you is upset about them anymore. You may benefit from the assistance of a therapist or coach.

Even doing a little bit of this work will help. It's possible, however, to actually be completely cleared of the past, and if you stick with the process for that long, a metaphysical shift happens. A clarity, a freshness, an in-rush of energy takes the place of all that had been previously muddying the water. It's a phenomenal thing. It's within reach for you as a couple to bring this to completion. Then as you continue to clear on a daily basis, nothing piles up anymore. To be in that clear of a space with your Beloved is worth all the effort it took to get there.

# Thank You for Bringing That Up

If you're going to have an agreement to bring every-thing up, you and your partner will most probably need to cultivate a changed attitude from the one you have now. Doing this practice, you're bound to learn things about yourself that are tough to hear. You were thinking you were being cool, but listening to your partner's point of view, you have to admit that, yes, you were instead being moody and a bit unkind. This comes as a ding to the ego. You're not as together as you thought, but really, isn't that the point? To grow out of having bad moods and taking them out on people? It often hurts when the truth's brought up—sometimes it's a pinprick; other times it pierces the heart.

Saying "Thank you for bringing that up," when our partner shares their truth, especially when it's difficult to hear, is a practice that will bypass the ego's interference. In that one phrase you are not only reinforcing to yourself that you want to hear things, even if they're difficult, so you can grow, but also acknowledging your partner's risk at sharing their truth, and that you welcome them doing so now and in the future.

"Thank you for bringing that up." Sometimes it will hurt to say that. Maybe during a conflict you got offended, and your ego doesn't feel particularly grateful. In that moment, if you thank your partner for bringing things up with you instead of with-holding, you're going to feel better. Sometimes you have to push yourself over that hill when you feel a little resentment. Remember your commitment to personal and spiritual growth.

Tantric relating grows through this process. When someone brings something up you did, you should be willing to examine your part in it, as it may be a pointer to how you need to mature and where you need to change. You might suddenly see a lifetime of conditioning, something you've been doing for twenty or thirty years—it isn't the way you want to be and you shouldn't be doing it any more.

This process clears the energy of the throat center, which is clogged from all the things we've never said, all the things it wasn't safe to say. When you're tantric relating, speaking truth and having your truth received, talking through everything, then everything you have to say with each other creates safety in your relationship.

Making agreements and thanking the other person for honoring them keeps the frequency between you clear and vitally alive. If instead you're cringing at the thought of what they might say, or they are hoping you won't bring things up, you're never going to get to the space of pure, vibrating clarity. Try it and you'll agree—it's the fast track of relating.

# Really, Until It's Done

You've made agreements to talk about things when they happen, or at least as soon as possible. You know that by letting misunderstandings fester, you run the risk of them mutating into something else altogether. Often, however, in your zeal to be happy, you will prematurely agree that an issue has been completely talked out. You nod, say everything's okay, and go on your merry way. Except that later in the day you find yourself being cranky, or you don't feel in the mood to make love, or find yourself sniping and angry. That's a sign that you're not done with everything that needed to be said. Sometimes talking about things until they're done may take a while.

Early on, I had an experience where something Greg said triggered me, and I realized I still had unfinished business from a year ago. I felt a little defensive bringing up an issue after so much time had passed, but since we have an agreement to talk about everything until it's done, that's what we did. It took several conversations for both of us to feel entirely clear, and when it was really done, it was like seeing the sun after a grim morning gloom.

In this example, if you had asked us, we would have both said the incident was done, but when I looked deeply, I could see that I still had charge that needed to be cleared. If it's not done for one person, it's not done for either of you. You can't be at the same frequency if one of you is holding on to something, no matter how miniscule or far in the past.

You might find that you and/or your partner are quick to want to declare something resolved, because it's uncomfortable not being done and you want to move on. That's understandable. This is also referred to as "sweeping things under the carpet" or "don't rock the boat." If and when you prematurely announce something complete, there remains a barely perceptible sensation that something's not quite right, which shows up as feeling distant from your partner. It decreases your desire for intimacy.

Sometimes you have to remind your partner, "Remember how we have an agreement to talk about everything until it's done? I want to bring up something. Is this a good time?" It's not always going to be pretty. Neither of you might want to get into a debate or be in the mood to dredge up old painful memories; you might find it triggering. Your partner might respond, "Really? Do you have to bring this up now? Aren't you done with that yet?" By focusing on the outcome—the energy clear and flowing freely between you—you become willing to do the work in order to make things better. The agreement is that you will continue until each person is done. Really done.

To make sure you're really done, another thing you can do to make space for the other person is to ask them, "What else? Are you sure, is there anything more? It feels like you're not quite done." You open yourself to receive your partner's truth, even if it stings.

How will you know when something's finished? Because you're making love beautifully. There's no sniping. You're both free to talk about whatever; you're having fun. That's how you know the communication's clear. If it's not, something's clogging the pipes, and it's up to you to unblock the line.

The learning curve can be steep, but once you learn to feel the energy and clear anything that's in the space between you, you will love the feeling. After that, it comes easily and becomes the only way to live, in complete clarity and in the present moment. Tantric relating is when the two of you are completely free and open with no unfinished business between you.

# Space to Be Upset

Tantric relating teaches us to give another person space to be upset. Women especially have been socialized to be so codependent that we rush in and try to fix our partner's feelings before they've even had a chance to feel them. Your partner's unhappiness can be so distressing to you that you try all kinds of strategies: denial that anything is wrong, premature forgiveness, or shaming them for having feelings at all. "That shouldn't bother you!"

In order to relate tantrically in a way that supports a soulmate relationship, you'll need to allow your partner their space to be upset, without interference. This can be difficult especially if you've come from a challenging childhood and aren't yet able to count on secure love, but practicing it will build strength in you and your partnership. If your partner's unsettled they have a right to their feelings. They deserve to deal with their inner experience alone and separate from you. I admit it can feel threatening.

Let me give you an example. Greg and I stopped by the Ventura County Fair on our way home from a day of sightseeing and were entering the grounds from the parking lot.

Greg reported, "Something triggered me and I was instantly in a bad mood. I didn't want to talk. I wanted to be pissed off. Catherine said something like, 'It's a nice day. I'm glad we're here.' I don't know why it did, but that bugged me. It seemed she barely knew that I was upset.

"I think I was in the porta potty when I came to my senses, and I said to myself, 'What the hell am I doing? This is a nice day. I do not want to be upset.' I pulled myself together and went back to her and I said, 'Wow, that was really bad. I'm sorry.' She said, 'That's okay. I knew you'd be back.'"

This example shows how if you're able to not take it personally and just wait a little while, the other person often gets ahold of themselves. You give them their space to return to the loving, independent person you know them to be.

Someone really wise once defined a successful relationship as one where only one person is crazy at a time. This means that occasionally you'll have to stand up and be the "sane one" because your partner is emotional and not at their best. You rise up as a rock of support for them. If the other person's momentarily unhinged and you know it's not because of anything you've said or done, you can give them their space, trusting that they'll return to you later. It helps to know that another person is holding space for you to be upset, and will be there for you when you come back to yourself.

# Praise, Thanks, and Flirting

Who in the world has ever said, "Please stop saying nice things about me. I've had enough"? No one. Who doesn't like to receive praise? In relationships, partners have often gotten into a habit of pointing out what's "wrong" with the other person: what we don't like and how they're not living up to our expectations, often communicated in a subtly disguised "just being helpful."

John and Julie Gottman, the psychologists who hook people up to electrodes and measure what actually works, found that in relationships between happy couples, the individuals are saying nice things to each other five times to the one time they have some sort of criticism. Every time you say, "Could you please clean up a bit more after yourself in the kitchen?" there will need to be five incidents of praise. Five to one!

This is a math equation few of us make use of, but it's something that can begin improving your relationship(s) immediately. Consciously remembering to make positive statements raises everyone's mood. Here are three action steps to get started on right away, and best of all—they're fun!

## Praise

When you're busy looking for things to praise about your partner, it's easy once you get going. You can praise their appearance: "You look hot in those pants." You can admire how they handle things: "The way you talked with Charlie was so powerful. I was proud of you." There are their achievements at work, that they stay fit, and their kindness with people. There's the all-purpose "I love you; you're awesome." How many more can you come up with?

## Thanks

Thanks and showing appreciation makes people feel good, both the one giving the thanks and the one receiving. Certainly in the outside world we hear that we don't make much of a difference. To come home to a warm nest where our partner is praising and thanking us is part of creating a soul-mate relationship.

You can thank your partner for being in your life, for showing up and being a good person. "Thank you for taking the garbage out. I really appreciate it." "Thanks for taking care of our family." Greg and I thank each other for our morning exercise: "Thanks for taking that walk with me." We even thank each other after we have sex: "Thank you. That was so beautiful." How often do you express your gratitude?

## Flirting

You may have had effective flirting skills when you were dating, but like most people, have forgotten to exercise them after you've been with someone for a while. Maybe you think it's not so easy to flirt when you've been hanging out together on the couch in your joggers, exchanged morning breath, and had more than a few spats. That's conventional thinking, and prone to make you blame your partner for why you're not making love any more.

If you want sex in your relationship, you'll want to remember to acknowledge your partner's sexiness. The best definition I've heard of flirting is that it's letting the other person know you see their sex appeal, especially if you're not going to act on it. It doesn't mean you're going to have sex now or later. It could—it's always fun to have the possibility hanging in the air. You make an acknowledgment of the other person's attractiveness in some cute way, a fun way, or even just through your energy.

If you're not going to praise, thank and flirt with your partner, who is? Answer: someone else, or no one. If your partner is going to get enough love in this lifetime, don't you want to be the one to provide it? You want them to be radiantly happy and to acknowledge that they're in their dream relationship. These small, easy-to-do actions go a very long way.

# When in Doubt, Touch

Touch is all-important for tantric relating. Tantrikas practice reminding ourselves that we live in bodies not just our heads, and that we want to relate to our Beloved from an embodied awareness not just from our minds analyzing everything. A mind in full-bore analysis mode can destroy even the best relationship. Nonverbal communication and touch speak louder than words.

It's true that we need to make agreements to talk about everything and continue the conversation until it's done. Yet sometimes you get stuck and the discussion is spiraling downward, and you don't know how to make it stop. At these times it's good to take a time-out and return later to finish. It's good for your bodies to connect for a few moments, placing a hand on the other's knee or arm as a way to communicate wordlessly, "I care for you. I know we're having trouble right now, but I want to work this out."

Your bodies will remember your connection even if you don't. For a moment, you won't be lost in your head arguing, coming up with points to make your case. When you settle into your body and reconnect in a friendly, loving way, your anxiety will lessen and your breath will slow down. Put your hand on their shoulder or arm, and simply connect. This will help the conversation veer away from two egos fighting to "Hey, we're a couple. We're going through this together. Let's breathe and let our bodies communicate." A simple gesture like this can often help guide the two of you out of the most difficult situations.

There's a great book called *How to Improve Your Marriage Without Talking About It* by Dr. Patricia Love (New York: Three Rivers Press, 2007). I once saw her speak, and she's quite charismatic and dynamic. The book isn't essential reading, but it does offer actual scientific studies that show that sometimes if you're in a difficult place in your relationship, if you will just reach out and reconnect with the other person through touch, the conversation will become easier. This is quite profound and useful information.

Bodies are often smarter than we are. When you get in a stuck space with your Beloved, touch. When you want to express affection, touch. When you want to offer support, congratulations, or difficult news, connect through gentle physical contact. Whenever you're in doubt about what to do, share your love through the gift of your touch.

# Relating Romantically

Conventional culture offers tried-and-true symbols to message that you're seeking romance: candles, flowers, low lighting, soft music, chocolates, delightful scents, delicious bites of forbidden food. All these things communicate "I'm wanting to relate romantically," and a tantric lover will make liberal use of them.

As a society, we've agreed that some places are more romantic than others. We usually imagine taking a stroll by the beach together, often at sunset. We picture dimly lit cafes serving French food and wine. Each couple will designate other locales as romantic depending on their histories, but one thing we all agree on is that the bedroom is a prime place for love, sex and romance. To relate romantically, you want to invest time and energy to make your bedroom beautiful. Once when I was talking about this on a podcast, the host said, "I'm going to go home and take the work papers out of the bedroom." That's a good idea! You want to create a dream space for romantic intimacy.

Romantic relating is also expressed nonverbally through slow, sensuous touch. You create a cocoon of safety for your partner: You can trust me; I will not make fun of you. You cuddle up together offering nurturing and softness. Romantic intimacy has to do with "I love the way you express yourself; I love your sexual expression." You communicate through your open heart, through loving touch.

Romantic relating also involves sexuality. We're looking for passion. We want to feel our energies rise. When we think of romantic ways of expressing sexuality, it most often is soft and slow and may take hours. At other times we may prefer lust and quickies, but for romance we want to gaze into our lover's eyes and take our time.

You want to consider not only what we as a culture agree on as romantic symbols, signs, and gestures. You also want to meditate on what puts you in the mood. What reminds you that your relationship is special and unique? Remember when you two were first in love—you felt as if no one's ever been in love as much as this. Wrap that silky blanket around you. Share memories from those early days. Help each other get into a space of romantic intimacy: We are a special couple; we are special to each other. You want to have a sense of your own power—you can create romantic intimacy.

# The Sky's the Limit

A relationship is never going to be a finished commodity if you stay alive and growing. It's true that familiarity can make things seem stale, and either of you could go to sleep. When we saw those types of relationships as kids or as singles, fear loomed in us that we might end up like that. I doubt anybody dreams of a relationship that's going downhill. Make a commitment that you're going to grow, and really go for it.

Whether or not your relationship stays vibrant will depend on your commitment to relate to each other as manifestations of the divine. It is contingent on agreeing to talk about everything, and being a big enough person to listen to ways you've been unkind or hurtful. It's an essential component of enlightened relating to bring things up right away, when they happen, and to talk about them until they're done. As you continue to grow, you'll become increasingly sensitive to the state of the energy between you and your partner. You'll find you'll want to clear everything current and past because even the slightest being "out" feels unbearable.

Osho said we have until our last breath to continue to grow and evolve. That can be the same with your relationship, that your relationship will continue to evolve, becoming more loving, kinder, more generous, less reactive, and less judgmental. It can also get juicier, sexier, and more alive as we get older. That can be your reality if you choose it. You can, in the same way as you made a commitment to your own growth, make a commitment to the growth of your relationship.

What we are advocating in this book is keeping the space between yourself and another person clear. Sometimes this will mean working through difficult stuff—sadness, resentment, jealousy, insecurity—in tantra we view it all as divine. Allowing the feelings to come up and sharing them in a way that creates more trust, until the process is done. Living in our bodies and sharing our healing touch. Remembering how amazing it is that this person has chosen to be in partnership with us (for whatever length of time) and expressing our gratitude frequently. Living these practices will show up in lovemaking where there's nothing in the way, the bodily expression of love flowing freely.

In *Tantric Dating*, the secrets of why you haven't found love and how to find it are explained. *Tantric Mating* teaches how to be in partnership and create your perfect soulmate relationship. This book, *Tantric Relating*, has been about how you can communicate both verbally and non- to keep the love fires burning.

If you both have the desire to grow personally and spiritually as much as you can in this lifetime, you'll someday arrive at the place where you find you've created the intimate relationship of your dreams. This is possible for you. I wholeheartedly want to encourage you to keep working on your personal and spiritual growth because perfect love is possible for you—the sky's the limit.

# TANTRIC RELATING EXERCISES

# EXERCISE #1: Envisioning Your Lover as the God or Goddess They Truly Are

One tantric exercise you can practice at home is to envision your lover as the god or goddess they truly are. That may seem a bit farfetched in today's world, as modern lovers are all too aware of what is "wrong" with their partner. Constantly bombarded with images of what the perfect lover looks like, talks like, kisses like, and makes love like, we compare and analyze and find our partners not measuring up. Since it is hard for a mere human being to live up to these two-dimensional fantasy figures, most of us experience our lovers (and ourselves) as lacking in the love department.

But what if we didn't focus on what we thought was wrong, but on what is right? What if we imagined the real person underneath their skin and their annoying habits? What if we pictured our Beloved as their essential nature and allowed ourselves to honor their lovingness, their vulnerability, and their attempts at becoming a better person?

When we imagine our partner as whole and perfect instead of fragmented and flawed, it becomes impossible to abuse, degrade, or dehumanize the other person. If they are by definition an equal, we cannot cultivate a condescending, contemptuous attitude. On the contrary, we view them with the gaze of a deity who is one of tenderness, clarity, and passion. Seeing our self as whole and perfect, our partner becomes a mirror of that perfection.

Ancient Tantric Buddhists practiced seeing the man as a male Buddha and the woman as a female Buddha, and therefore, lovemaking became two Buddhas making love. The lovers practiced seeing each other as pure energy spontaneously expressing itself in embodied being.

Today, you can have fun with these practices. Certain tantric gods and goddesses have red or blue skin that could be fun to imagine. Some tantric texts describe the body of the lover as translucent or luminous like a rainbow. Think how delightful this could be to envision while stroking your lover's skin!

The tantrikas saw their feelings of passion and desire as having a transcendent aspect, and their mutual attraction as ultimately motivated by a spiritual impulse toward ecstasy. To move in the direction of an attitude like this can help transform the negative messages most of us were brought up with concerning sex. By envisioning our Beloved as divine, it is possible to increase the love in the world and to elevate our ordinary sex acts to acts of worship.

# EXERCISE #2: Do You Want to Tell the Truth?

It may seem scary or daunting to move from a conventional relating style of being positive and not talking about things to tantric relating where you are living in and honoring the truth. It's okay to be where you are in the process—it's more important to tell yourself the truth that you're not ready. First, list the things you're not eager to share with anyone: stories from your past, health concerns, times you screwed up, or politically incorrect feelings such as jealousy, insecurity, and anger.

1.



2.

3.

4.

There also may be things you don't want to hear from your partner. There's an old joke that relates to the differences in the way men and women are socialized: A woman asks her partner to share his feelings, asking him over and over until finally he says, "Okay! I'll tell you how I'm feeling: I feel impotent at work, scared about the future, and I want to have sex with your best friend." "Not that!" yells the woman. "I don't want to hear about that!"

What of your partner's truth would be hard for you
to hear?

1.

2.

3.

4.

# EXERCISE #3: Making Agreements

Tantric relating is about making agreements with your partner that you both want to live in an environment of trust, truth, respect, and open communication about what's going on for each of you. It sets completely new ground rules for any relationship.

What tantra offers is not the same as conventional wisdom to smile all the time and hope everything's fine. A lot of people who are working on themselves think it's about being positive no matter what and taking things to a higher level, creating what we call spiritual bypass where people aren't living their truth. They aren't sharing if they're sad, jealous, or upset about what was just said because that wouldn't be upbeat. Resentment builds, and then they are surprised when the relationship starts to tank.

It's a big commitment to make an agreement to talk about everything. It will change your life. If you're not ready at this time, that's okay. Just watch what your results are as you continue on your growth path. You can move slowly toward greater disclosure if that works better for you. One hundred percent commitment, however, is the place where magic begins.

1. Are you ready to make an agreement to talk about everything?

2. When it happens?

3. Until it's done, and the energy is flowing freely again?

4. Are you willing to clear the past? Both your own and the relationship's?

# EXERCISE #4: Clean Sweep

For pure tantric relating you'll need to do a major housecleaning. Anything still bugging you from the past keeps you from being able to be present with what's really happening. An example might be if you grew up with a father who was always criticizing you, you imagine your partner is putting you down when they are not. The past mistreatment has not been resolved, and you're seeing your partner through the eyes of that little person you once were.

This clean sweep can be done in psychotherapy or in any of the other processes mentioned previously. You can also journal, create art about it, or join a therapy or Twelve-step group. Many people are willing and skilled in how to help you with "cleaning out the basement." The sooner you start, the sooner you'll be able to live in the present moment instead of being mired in the past.

Some places I'm still stuck are:

1.


2.


3.


4.


If you're currently in a relationship, the two of you most probably have unresolved issues from the past: arguments that were never resolved, talks about your sex life that need to happen, differences in style in spending habits, child-raising, and future goals. All these matters that need to be settled keep you from being able to have clear, flowing energy between the two of you.

Past issues that we as a couple need to talk through to completion are:

1.


2.


3.


4.

# EXERCISE #5: Raise the Bar

You learned about the Gottman's formula of five statements of praise and gratitude to one correction or request. What if you took this on as a daily discipline to praise, thank, or flirt with your partner five times a day?

There are an unlimited number of things to **Praise** about your partner. Here are a few to get you started— circle the ones you want to use and add your own.

- Their hot body
- Financial independence
- Their kind heart
- Talents and skills, even little ones
- Their competence
- Good taste in music or movies
- Intelligence
- Good values
- The way they contribute to you and the family
- Responsibility

It's not hard to **Thank** your partner when you recognize their divine nature. Here are a few items to expand on and share:

- That you show up for our relationship
- For taking care of your body
- That you accept me, warts and all
- Picking up after yourself
- That you share in the household chores
- Accepting my family
- For lovemaking
- Being an upstanding human being
- For talking a walk with me
- Being a giver instead of a taker

Figuring out how to **Flirt** is really fun. Get creative!

- When you're out grocery shopping, pat them on the butt.
- Tell them frequently how arousing you find them.
- Look in their eyes just a little bit longer and raise your eyebrows and smile.

- Buy a silly mug that says something like "World's Greatest Lover."

- Order surprise gifts of sexy thongs, especially if their body is unconventionally beautiful.

- Remind them of romantic moments from your shared past.

- Touch, touch, and more touch.

# EXERCISE #6: What Do We Mean by "Spiritual Relationships?"

"WIIFM" is the primary motivator for many people in their relationships. WIIFM is a marketing term for "What's in It for Me?" We have been taught to value people for how good they will look on our arm, how close they come to our fantasy of the ideal lover, or how we imagine they will fulfill our desires. It's about how it all looks, right? Except that when we focus on the outside, nobody is going to be good enough because everyone is flawed. Everybody. This is why we love the tabloids—we get to see seemingly perfect celebrities with their defects hanging out.

One characteristic of a spiritual relationship is that instead of focusing on the other person's exterior, we focus on the perfection within. Just as we all have not-so-beautiful parts on the outside, we all have a perfect core at our center. When we want our relationship to have a spiritual component, we attempt to keep our attention on this perfection within, rather than concentrating on what's outside.

The great tantra master Osho once said regarding relationships, "The Other is always right." I was stunned when I first heard this. Like most people, I had been constantly pointing out when I was right and my partner was wrong, all in the name of "communicating honestly." In retrospect, it was all a thinly disguised power struggle.

I argued with Osho's statement in my mind and then decided to see what I could learn from it. As a technique, I recommend it highly. You don't have to agree with it to experiment. Practice interpreting that the other was right and you were wrong next time you are reviewing a fight or disagreement. The ego spends all its time proving that it is superior. See what happens from the perspective of love.

When you begin this discipline of seeing what is right about the other person rather than what is, according to you, wrong, you may start to experience your partner as your teacher, or guru. Some of the other attributes of spiritual relationships that people have mentioned are placing a high value on listening, integrity, emotional openness, sensitivity, truth, having a raise-the-bar attitude, and having a passion for learning and growing.

When people's lives are dedicated to something higher than just getting their own needs met, their relationships will follow suit. This can show up as a dedication to making the world a better place by working for the environment, helping kids, or serving some other higher calling. Your relationship will be dedicated to something more important than merely trying to get your needs met, and this is what we call a spiritual relationship.

# Acknowledgments

Thanks to Margaret Drewry Walsh, Sandra Sloss Giedeman, Lilly Penhall, Kimberly Grace, Abbe Kantor Jaye, and my dream-come-true husband, Greg Lawrence.

Thanks to the inspiring example set by the following tantric couples. While not all of these people identify as "tantric" – what I mean by the word is that their partnership serves the world and that the spiritual dimension of relationships is acknowledged and lived by them: Diana and Michael Richardson, Alex and Allyson Grey, John and Julie Gottman, Peter Rengel and Donna Spitzer, Tom Kenyon and Judi Sion, Sasha and Anne Shulgin.

Thanks to the many teachers and systems who teach about the importance of clearing: David Schnarch, PhD, Human Awareness Institute, NLP, Osho Multiversity, The Tech, Toltec Shamanic Recapitulation, and Twelve-step programs.

And most of all on-my-knees gratitude to Osho, the great tantra master.

# About the Author

Catherine Auman, LMFT (Licensed Marriage and Family Therapist) is a spiritual psychotherapist and the Director of The Transpersonal Center. She has advanced training in traditional psychology as well as the wisdom traditions. Catherine lived for a year at the Osho ashram in India – a full-time immersion in tantra and meditation – and she has studied and practiced tantra, love, sex, intimacy, and seduction with numerous teachers. She lives in Los Angeles with her husband, Greg Lawrence, with whom she teaches tantra and relationship enhancement.

# Connect with Catherine Auman

| | |
|---|---|
| Websites: | catherineauman.com |
| | thetranspersonalcenter.com |
| Facebook: | catherineaumanlmft |
| Instagram: | @catherineauman |
| Youtube: | catherineauman |
| Eventbrite: | thetranspersonalcenter |

# Create the Sex, Love and Romance of Your Dreams with *The Tantric Mastery Series*

Imagine yourself in a perfect soulmate relationship full of sex, love and romance. Open yourself to love and awareness.

These three beautiful books teach you how.

- *Tantric Dating*
- *Tantric Mating*
- *Tantric Relating*

**Buy Now online or at your favorite retailer**

**Print, Ebook, or Audiobook**

# Works by Catherine Auman

**Books**

*Tantric Mastery Series*

> *Tantric Relating: Relationship Advice to Find and Keep Sex, Love and Romance*

> *Tantric Mating: Using Tantric Secrets to Create a Relationship Full of Sex, Love, and Romance*

> *Tantric Dating: Bringing Love and Awareness to the Dating Process*

*Mindful Dating: Bringing Loving Kindness to the Dating Process*

*Guide to Spiritual L.A.: The Irreverent, the Awake, and the True*

*Shortcuts to Mindfulness: 100 Ways to Personal and Spiritual Growth*

*Fill Your Practice with Managed Care*

**Workshops**

*Tantra: The Science of Creating Your Soulmate*

*Tantra: The Foundations of Conscious Touch*

*Tantric Secrets about Women*

*Tantric Secrets about Men*

*Tantra and the Psychedelics of Sex*

*MDMA and Couples Therapy*

**Audio Recordings**

*Tantric Embodiment Induction*

*Deeply Relaxed*

*Awareness Breathing*

Made in the USA
Middletown, DE
20 March 2023

27179680R00066